Beautiful Wilderness

Jean Bonnin

Jean Bonnin

Jean Bonnin was born in Lavaur, in the Tarn in France. He is a novelist, poet, artist, and musician who now lives in South West Wales.

Beautiful Wilderness
An Original Publication of Red Egg Publishing
An imprint of Red Egg International
First published in the UK by Red Egg Publishing
in 2017
www.redeggpublishing.com

Copyright © Jean Bonnin 2017

Jean Bonnin has asserted his moral right to be identified as the author of this book

Cover design: Red Egg Publishing

British Library Cataloguing-in-Publication Data

A catalogue record for this book is available upon request from the British Library

ISBN: 978-0-9571258-8-9

This book is sold subject to the condition that it shall not, by way of trade or otherwise, be lent, re-sold, hired out, or otherwise circulated without the publisher's prior consent in any form of binding or cover other than that in which it is published and without a similar condition including this condition being imposed on the subsequent purchaser

Contents

One Hand Clapping	page 10
She Dances I	page 12
Nostalgia	page 14
Marshmallow Moon	page 16
Listen to Ladybirds	page 18
The Gift	page 20
Split the Sky	page 22
Beautiful Wilderness	page 26
Poetry	page 28
What the Fuck Happened to Monday	page 30
The Moon and Me	page 32
You	page 34
Tomorrow-land	page 38
Puffs of Smoke	page 40
The Feast	page 42
Devils and Angels	page 44
Flowers Disturb	page 48
Turning of Clocks	page 50
Dalí's House	page 52

Pictures in My Mind	page 56
The Red Painting	page 60
The Cigarette	page 63
Word Zoo	page 64
The Bird's Last Cry	page 68
Unwieldy	page 70
Bright and Warm	page 76
Endless Ocean	page 78
Telephone Ring	page 80
Marching In Time	page 82
Rennes-le-Château	page 84
Plug Yourself In	page 86
A *La Perdrix* Wedding	page 88
The End of Summer In France	page 90
Good Holes	page 92
Cool Whispers	page 96

One Hand Clapping

Do you remember
When they told us to live our lives
According to the sunrise

How many times
Have you let beautiful moments slip
through your fingertips
And never quite let the words reach
your lips

I can see the dawn coming up again
As I wander through my orchard days
All brown and golden in shade and
temperament
As I tread crisply along my unknown
path

If I give you my yesterdays
Your eyes will widen as you smile
If you give me your tomorrows

I will sculpt you a form as yet unseen
Soft to the touch and pleasing to the
eye

You remember when you heard the
song of the bird
Whose name escapes me now
It filled you with such happiness
And yet you were frightened of
listening too long

Well reach out while it is in front of
you
Before it dissolves into a one hand
clap
And before you become the audience
applauding an
empty stage

She Dances I

She dances with eyes closed and head gently tilted
In her dimly lit room to the sound of the pelting rain
But all she really hears is the music
The music coming from out of her mirror
Where people are dancing and swaying just out of sight
They toss back their heads and laugh
And spill their champagne and laugh some more
They are elegant and beautiful and confident
And though every evening they remain hidden
She knows they are there
And she knows it is only a matter of time

Before they invite her into their world
And so each night she dances and sways
To the faint music
Until the moment
She can escape her monochrome existence
For the colourful land
She can almost touch

Nostalgia

The sunlight stole my nostalgia
Took my youth and twisted it into
cynical resignation
My dreams and darkness were
intertwined in those days
I just woke up one day to a rusty
mirror and a thankless task

I never used to notice the birdsong
My thick curtains protecting me from
the daylight air-raids

We would nod silently to each other
happy in the knowledge that we were
the only ones awake on the planet

Secrets that presented themselves to
us alone

I could sometimes hear a piano
playing in the distance
As another candle spluttered its
requiem

Marshmallow Moon

The swaying trees
Chinese whisper their thoughts upon the world
As I carve my nonsense for posterity
With a knife, a pen and tied-together parchment
Tomorrow is the unobtainable dream

In silent meadows landing-craft wait for eyes to turn away
As we sit with the hedgerow as our shield
From a world that stomps its time
To fight the infinite mirror on the horizon

If I could dance with the happiness of the unknowing
I would do so

If I could sing to the careless frivolity
of lady luck
I would shout out loudly my feelings
and my words

Roll on sweet breath of morning
warmth
Yellow sun and marshmallow moon
Rounded hilltop and splashing wave
All for a lover's kiss in the stinging rain

Listen to Ladybirds

I don't want to climb a tree
I don't want to purchase a priest
Together we can do anything
Listen to ladybirds sing

Fortune favours the rivers
Through my soul
Eating away the molluscs
In my brain

Tomorrow drinks from infinite
waterfalls
Summer sun
Spring-coil-ready
To explode
Winter drinker
Autumn thinker just for fun

Sing drink love

Grating teeth
Joker-poker
In the fires of eternity
You me us we
Before it becomes a blur in the sea

For time is time
And you know something you cannot tell
Take it and make it
Shake it
But don't ever break it or forsake it

Revived with hope of a thousand wishes
In streams of everlasting everything
Think about it
Everybody dance
Hold your hands up to the sky and dance
Before the music-birdsong-humming fades

The Gift

I've got a drawer full of t-shirts
From the memories I used to know
With a bookcase of forgotten pages
From when I had all the time in the world
My wallpaper hides the depths
Behind my ice-stung-stained existence
Collecting automobiles and used toilet rolls
For something I could stick together
To make into a den
A den with a double-sided certitude
Swallows and amazons, hiccoughs and dragonflies,
And tree-climbing preachers – all traded in
For supermarket trolley visionaries
The crowds line the streets like the trees used to do

Flip-book photo-movement fakery
Soothing the people into dangerously
fearful animation

Tomorrow never knows and yesterday
is forgotten
As the gift of the present is always a
stone's throw away
From a still-frame-caught shattered
light bulb

I can see the lighthouse in the
distance
Guiding the darkness onto the rocks
So as to spiral our futures
Into smithereens

Split the Sky

Split the sky with the sharpened bones made from a thousand forgotten hopes for a future filled with the poetry and rhythms of the waters that dash against the rocks and splice the spray into my pale stinging winter cheeks.
Alive she cried, I'm alive she cried – able to see through the mists to a day I believed would be when I was too young to think there was any other way. A memory crosses the mind of a time when the luxury existed in not knowing, not understanding, not thinking, pure being and fun and laughter and the strawberry lips from floppy jam sandwiches.
Pain was a grazed knee; not the end of light in sodden half-lit grey concrete

streets. Up-raised collars can only protect you so far – from the paltry grime and the ticking of time and the plastic lessons and the unnecessary token-filled lies of everyday avoidable and yet unavoidable interactions. Save hope, long live hope. Don't let the bastards turn the dial down to make the exquisite sounds become wallpaper. Don't let your clothes reflect your fears. Don't let sanity rule in this all-too-easily forgotten beautiful chaos. Sing … sing … sing … scream it all out. And raise a glass of milk and whisky to the protectors of our imagination, our colourful crayon drawings and chocolate that melts in your hand.

Shout across the stream with the wobbly glistening half-submerged rocks, and step cautiously over to your lover wrapped in his scarf with his held out hand. He loves you and the world will catch up one day… Catch up with soaking turn-ups, smiles, un-questioned trust and love. Cos that's all there is, and it is that which trumps all else... Love is all – love is all – love is all... Everybody sing to restored hope ... and let the world begin again... Begin again... Bang-bang... begin again.

Beautiful Wilderness

I'll drive you out to the distant light
To where the trees are replaced
With desert and long horizons

I'll take you to a beautiful wilderness
To where the sun will melt your sorrow
And where the clouds will make a thousand different pictures

We shall sit and drink our wine
As the desert winds grow
In a place where the native peoples played

I'll take you to a beautiful wilderness
Sun, moon, laughter and shadows –
emptiness and hope

For a future that is both solitary and
collective

And I'll show you who I truly am
Desert night, hologram
In a place where the sky has no end...

And hold me in the desert glow
Touch me by the firelight
Sing me songs about the everyday
When I'm not quite sure what to say

And I'll take you
Take you to a beautiful wilderness

Poetry

Poetry comes from other planets
Distant misty mythical places
Where sense is defined by essence
and feeling,
Emotion and meaning
And not solely by the boxed in
definitions
Given by dictionaries and stilted
tradition

Rhythm, melody, allusion and love
Outweigh any understanding derived
from the surface
Poetry as with love should be seen
through the prism of
Matryoshka-like secrets upon secrets
To be revealed with each new wave of
consideration

Meaning is within the mind of the beholder...
Often hidden within plain view

What the Fuck Happened to Monday

What the fuck happened to Monday
He was always somewhere
Always somewhere doing something
Tat and jive descendants
Formulating and postulating in whirly
prose
Like the phases of the moon

As was I – I was always somewhere
doing something
That was reassuring somehow
Like a lost soul in desert dunes
Kicking sand in the faces of the now

One day our paths will cross –
That's what I told myself
Uncontrived, like a joker of
happenstance

Maybe on a subway with matching Greek newspapers:
A doorkeeper to the strange and *anonyme*

Something would be exchanged – a look, a nod,
A signal to the acceptance of the other, of otherness... then gone
And so it is: gone
Forever gone – the moment, the time;
The missed opportunity which never existed

Whatever happens next – real or perceived
Dust particle or imagined imagery –
Whatever happens next... it won't,
It simply will not, be boring

The Moon and Me

The moon strikes down on blue water
The time will come or so they say for reflection
And deep laughter

But I'm not there in a sudden way
I remain on the edge of strong currents

The moon journeys down to this rock of mine
And the trees spell out their promise
And I will love in this way of mine
For there is no other

The dawn will come along with the mist
Blessed with the mystery of tomorrow
And I shall leave this rock of mine

Forgetting myself and my sorrow

And the moon will always shine for me

You

You're the most beautiful thing
that somebody without faith could say
that god created

The sound of an accomplished mouth-
organ
on a sunny jetty in the early morning
in an Irish fishing village
The water splashing against your
dangling legs
and your hair – I can never forget your
hair
You catch the light in your eyes
and your palms are open and upward
And I'm happy here with – with you
And tomorrow will have to wait and it
may never come
the way that I feel now

You utter words from your own made up language –
and nothing can touch me, us, you

And the world could be so much better
But not than we are now, here
And I would do anything, and will do, and do do – and I love you

And I'm sorry for the daily scourges that have no importance
But we see further than that
The world is a ball
That we pick up and throw to each other bare foot in the sand dunes

And Nikki Sudden sings and Iggy dances
A camera clicks and captures once again
And it is us my dear who are the film or the book or the life

That makes me happy – that makes me what I am

And this is our life – and I thank you for that

Tomorrow-land

The crescent-moon-sparkled-foam
Of the rushing tide
Gazed at from behind
Unforgiving panes
Of private hell
Is a release from the blank page
And the raging solitude of night

The ashtray spills with half-forgotten thoughts
Its stillborn moments in truth
As the solitary drip from the half-empty bottle
Slides to its demise
Amongst the incomplete sentences
And unwritten words
To a tomorrow that never arrives

The future through the window

And across the water
Drips with the golden
Honey-suckle morning mists
Autumn hay bale shafts of light
Dance upon gently blown
Fields of wheat

And tomorrow is a land
Where mystery is held
In the out-stretched palm
Of a beautiful woman
Walking gently away
Towards the banks
And waters
Of a new day

Puffs of Smoke

Hey Mr Preacher man
With your wide-brimmed ideas
Telepathic revelations
And starched indignation
Crying wolf for a handful of beans
Dealing in magic and puffs of smoke
Selling snake oil to the needy and deranged
- Pick a card any card
- Not that one... I can stop the rising of the sun

Button fixation
Supermarket trolley
Whiplash madman playing musical chairs
With mounds of sand and dice-throwing prejudice

Am-dram war pigs from asylum central
Psychic TV detectives asking
- Who luvs yer baby?
Baldness is an advantage in hotter climes

The cave paintings used to be wiser than this
Messages from our ancestors
But don't bring the hillside
Bury yourself inside
Tunnel in
Take food and bones
And await the ending of the world

The Feast

The feast of the forgotten few
The banquet to the distorted mind
The celebration of the revellers and
Worshippers of distracted
inconvenience
Was the scene that finally broke me
And with insane fireside abandon
Allowed me to peel away the masks
Both contrived and unidentified
And burn them in a stamping whirling
frenzy

The visions came almost instantly
And made me laugh out loud
Like the pleasure of a crazed
Burning nobleman dancing amongst
the hot coals
Whilst being whisked away into
oblivion
And the music continued to play

As heads were thrown back in merriment
And intense inebriation
The dancers span-spun around so quickly
That their long hair created silhouette circles
And all the while I continued to discard
My outer layers of being until I was swept upwards
And disappeared like a graceful bird of legend
Into one of my own visions

Devils and Angels

The angel said to the devil
You're a liar and a cheat
And the devil said to the angel – so
are you

Do this do that – don't don't
Yeah do it, go on you know you can…

You are the devil, the black bird, the
dying crow –
you have everything…
Liar, cheat – we must not be swayed
by cheap
gimmicks
and your oh so holy yes-you-cans
Be gone dark ember of deception –
you have no interest
here

Then they took a head, a random
head, and they spoke...
They found the head to be of many
channels and corridors and openings
as yet not travelled.
And they were curious –
but this was merely an aside,
and was not dwelled upon more than
fleetingly.
And they spoke to, within and
around...

Take it, take it.
Come come with me... Dance to the
visions of Huxley;
Sip and spill from Burrough's goblet.
Nooooo; stay away from such
waveries
and blind psychological alleyways.
Dance to the craziness of all pervasive
knowing.
Knowledge is entrance, lysergic the
key.

You're going to see skies of azure and
temples of delicacy
and intrigue.
You will see the self and peel back the
layers of clay fortress –
to reveal the majesty of revelation
in its translucent finger-tipped
outreach.

You are death, and you will be death.
And you will be a fool to follow the
path
that is laughingly known as
knowledge.
Wisdom is a one-edged sword facing
inwards for eternity.
You will hold mammon's beating
breast in your cupped trembling
hands.
Do not enter the door to this fool's
paradise that encapsulates
the screams of a thousand pulsating
indecisions
from the dark side

This is all jest and sleight of hand.
Who in their right mind would not
pass on into the final step

Where the candles are of the most
spell-binding beauty
Lighting up a room of infinite mirrors
Each containing a reassuring smile of
familiarity
And distant mystery.

...But it was never clear who was
saying what

Flowers Disturb

The bed is still warm
Night time flight to other planes
Where the sand stings the sea
And flowers disturb the meadow

Brightly coloured satin clichés
Scream pretty lifetime haunts
And yesterdays shall never sing
To swallows' swooping death dives

Fortunes and coal dust
Happy now
Safe for the laughter
On horizons which drip with lost hope
Encased in gelatine…
Could be honey
Nectar
Drowsy wishfulness

She lies and listens to the outside
traffic birdsong:
Double-parked squawking arrogance
Plumed desire for metal mating ritual
Strutting hubris
Rising to join the formation
For the journey towards the warmth

She turns on her pillow and sighs
As the doorpad clack
And the flapping in the street
Signal the slapping of waves
Over the oil slick pristine beaches
That we used to know

Turning of Clocks

He pulled his brain out with a skewer
and an empty thought
He looked around him, summer
sunshine in a can
Don't know where he's going to, put
his coat on and turned the screw
He had a house and garden, he
doesn't know what'll happen

He has seen the flash of time
The turning of clocks and walking in
line
Drops of water on his head
Make it easier to dream in bed

Tulips drooling by the fireside
Dog in a bucket and somewhere to
hide

Feng-shui nation and a satellite station
Lotus feet and a cool place to eat

But this could be the end of the line...

Dalí's House

The labyrinth divides the egg in two
But this is just a thought
In truth they are interchangeable
As is perception and memory
And the reliability of the mind

The Port bobs to the Mediterranean
breeze
Fishing shattered sparkling splintered
mirror glistening
Reflective little wooden boat blues
and greens
All seen from through the angled
mirror
At the end of the bed
Every morning he was the first
Spaniard to see the sun rise
Is what he said

The stuffed animals speak together
Now their keeper is dead
They talk of their hopes, dreams
And what they've seen – and general animal things

The studio's two unfinished paintings tantalise us
As Escher-like stairwells lead us both up and down
In and out
Until our minds pop
Into thinking that possibly we are but pieces
In an elaborate game
Trekking through a life that has gone
And that yet in a small way we are still part of

Sickness snatches the strong as it envelopes the meek
Death will take us, as with the flute playing frogs,

Into the dream world or into nothing at all

And then, possibly as a metaphor for everything,
It is all too quickly over
As we pass the long thin swimming pool
At the end of which is a banqueting table
Where Jesus and Mary Magdalene could have sat
Or with the swinging suspended serpent
Where Adam and Eve may have dined

And then out into a world
Which henceforth should be seen
Through more frivolous eyes

Pictures in My Mind

I can't draw
Daisy chains or concrete jungles
I have no perspective
In life I do, at least I hope I do

I can't see the wood for the planks
Not even the planks, the rectangles
My world is flat
Two-dimensional
Shapes are great but shading would
be better

I can see the pictures in my mind
They really are quite marvellous
Even if I somewhat immodestly say so
myself
I am really rather good you know

Up there with Hieronymus Bosch, Dalí and van Eyck
Unique I would say in my challenging
Somewhat confrontational use of colour
Slightly more real than surreal
A little more impression than Impressionist
And possibly less expressionistic
Than rather an expression of my inner-most
Reflections on post-modern angst
Either that or they're of flowers... flowers in my mind

In a parallel universe in a comparable evolutionary state
But where TVs, radios and computers don't exist
I am a world renowned painting performer
That is a primary source of entertainment, you know –
The painting performer

I sit on the stage of old theatres around the country
In front of audiences of several hundred
With my easel and my paints at hand, and I paint.
I paint.

It is all magnified and projected onto a large screen
So even those at the back of the auditorium
Can appreciate my deft little brushstrokes
And pointillist representations

Yes, I really am quite good
Known throughout the country
Interviewed by all the leading journals and magazines
And my paintings sell for a lot of money
And the demand far outweighs what I am able to produce

Ah yes, and perspective and depth
Are two of the things I am most
known for

But here in this life my world is flat
I drew a rather good circle once, a
circle inside a square it was
But I don't think it would have shaken
up the artwork
Even if I'd had the gumption to show
it to anyone
But difficult though it is to admit –
that's all it was
That's all it was
Arrrr… in the land of the blind the
one-eyed man is king
In a flat world I would be king –
Or at least principal artist to the king

The Red Painting

The red painting hangs silently
Between works of varying quality
Its lack of originality
Is both irritating and frustrating
There is nothing else red in the room
Even the lipstick of the smiling women
Some of whom don't know why
they're there
Is pale in comparison

The red painting bleeds its mediocrity
Onto my retinas
Forcing me to despise
Its inability even to be vulgar
Vulgarity would have been something
- at least it would have given me
something
Solid to latch onto

Next to the red painting is a piece of
work hanging
One and a half meters by half a meter
It consists of strips of torn up
newspapers
It is by the same artist as the red
painting
It equally leaves me cold
If there is anything inside me that is
moved
It is the feeling that I really must
purchase
A newspaper today…

Papier maché pointlessness
Suspended next to
Red unnecessariness

The red painting has achieved the
Miraculous position of being
At one and the same time
Both too red and not red enough…
The red painting lacks

Innovation, imagination, sincerity,
humour and love…

Two months later I visited the optician
And discovered that I am colour blind

I returned to the gallery and bought
the red painting
It now hangs in my house –
I have called it
The green painting

The Cigarette

The cigarette takes me between its
finger and thumb
And pinches me till I bleed
Smoke me you fucker it screams
Suck me to the end of my life
You love me
Sometimes you love me more than
you love yourself
The battle continues
Like a destructive lover's plate-
throwing incompatibility
Take me in your mouth, forget all else,
and fire me up
Smoking – in a certain place at a
certain time –
Makes me feel as though I only exist
within the lines of a David Bowie song

Word Zoo

Crocodile tears
Of pigeon fanciers
Over dog-eared books
From a cat-calling sister
With fishy motives
Who wolves down her meals
And squeals like a pig
When made to sing like a canary
Over the monkey she paid
For the stolen beetle
She'd heard about
Directly from the horse's mouth
Who was as slippery as an eel
When asked to reveal
The source of the old donkey she'd bought
From the snake in the grass
Who was a two-faced worm
And a supergrass who was

The tail that wagged the dog
Of the underworld and who
Sold her the pig in a poke in the first place
For a monkey instead of a pony
But it was all dented
Because he'd driven it
Like a bull in a china shop
And though you can't make
A silk purse from a sow's ear
She'd purchased it anyway
And naively put all her eggs
Into one basket
For a dinosaur
That quickly ended up
As dead as a dodo
But she couldn't come clean
Because she didn't want to do bird
Irrespective of having a flea in her ear
About having a frog in her throat
And a hoarse voice
Happily however
She ended up
As the worm that turned

And told the little ferret
That he was a weasel
And wanted back her king's ransom
To have her own day at the races
And celebrate with
A pint of mickey mouse

The Bird's Last Cry

The water plunges up towards me
Embalming fluid rushing up into my silence
Still, crashing torrents gasping into a desperation of waves
The gulls circle, like winged dolls

My stillness represents resolution not anguish
The rocks below me smile, captivating like cloud formations
To swoop gracefully rather than to plummet like a childhood dream
The gulls circle, like holy vultures

A scrap of newspaper ciphers past
Tomorrow's truths for yesterday's people
No longer my concern

Like Sirens the gulls are summoning
me

Blue and green merge
The coldness of air distracts me
The horizon tilts, pouring itself away
The last shrill cry of the birds –
nothing.

Unwieldy

The ceiling had tightened its grip around my head once again as the chanting
re-emerged…
The bulb swung on a piece of string and the dank bed glued itself to my consciousness – as autumn caped the room.
…Never lose sight – I told myself; lose that and they win. I took something to dull the pain. I got up and dressed.
But, that was much earlier…

I guess before I do anything else I should tell you where I'm at at the moment…Funny really but I don't really do this sort of thing…
Anyways, yeah, it's hard to explain really –

I guess the best thing to do is just tell
you about an average day...
Today for example.

I took the metro to the inner-skirts of
this...of this...PLACE.
I don't think I'm that happy at
present, but y'know, it's hard to tell.
The nuances have become so slight
these days, and y'know, the memories
are so distant now. Memories of
anything other than THIS.

I don't think they know you know –
I really don't think they know you
know.

I'm good at the game – in short
bursts.
I can sort of, you know, look like
someone who doesn't feel the way I
do.
But it needs concentration – I've gotta

build up to it, I couldn't do it
everyday.
A few times a month maybe.

Anyway, what was I saying. Yeah; an
average day of *dasein*. So, I
takes the metro to where the trees
are replaced by lamp-posts,
and where the buildings hide a million
different secrets;
where lonliness and crowds of people
are a juxtaposition
that has lowered the bar and become
the norm.
Unquestioned, as it is, cos it is the
overpowering zeitgeist
that has creeped and seeped into
every pore;
and it is as though it has always been
this way,
and in any case nobody remembers it
as ever having been different.
And the buildings shadow a million
secrets –

and there is much contact,
and yet there is none at all.
So, I took the train to this place –
and I walked and I walked, and the
grey water-washed sky was only a
slightly different shade
from the bricks that surrounded me...
Yet, I'm no artist, no genie from a
bottle;
a bottle of turpentine washed away
the colours that I was daubed in a long
time ago.

And I walked the streets, and crossed
over
pavements cracked and bleeding from
the still damp skies.
And I trod out a path and chose my
route carefully,
arbitrarily and maybe unwieldy –
unwieldy to the onlooker. But, there
were none,
NONE that counted, none that I
counted; none that counted on me.

There never were.
And my path, as I say, was deliberate.
Although
it may well have looked like a solitary man walking
a random route – it was I... and I chose my steps carefully
(I didn't count them, this time).

I went to the crossroads
where the traffic lights shone out their instructions
and turned left. Crossed over and took a side way,
round the corner and through the arch.

I was succumbing to my compulsion to spell out my way...
As I walked I spelt a word, WORDS, a sentence.
The curly parts of the letters were difficult in this gridline world.

But it mattered little I figured, as I
chose a cuboid typescript –
ancient computers and quadrangles.

And I walked and I walked, and I sang
to myself as I did –
I'm sure no one noticed me.
And I ended in the park –
the final 'curl' to the final letter.
My hours of walking, I had spelt out
the words
G-O-D-I-S-D-E-A-D-I-AM-GOD

Bright and Warm

The sun gets me up early these days
Bright and warm and needing sleep
The wind and the trees whispering
ancient histories

I've walked on rocks rounded by the
moon
And lain in bushes that have held my
body
And cradled my tune
Five senses I have and the sixth is for
you

As I walked in the square and the
Moonlight struck
I felt your hand touch my shoulder
I turned but you were gone

We lived in a mansion

Desolate and decayed
A tapestry of antiquity – beauty and dust

The radio played and then fell with the stars
I lit a cigarette
You drank to the night and the day and the night

We held the moment and each other in our arms

Endless Ocean

Streams of light
Glisten and dance
On sun-kissed ripples
On an ocean with no end
Under a sky the bluest of blue

Reflections are like questions
From a distant unlocked room
Waves and fragments
Give half-meanings to half-light
In a shadow-land of infinite
possibilities

Fishes are metaphors
In an incomplete poem
Turquoise, blue and golden rain
Scaled over like the cataract answers
Unformulated questions on a sea of
infinite tomorrows

And if I swim – what then?
Who shall save me
From the torrents and the whirlpools
Of all the stories (yet) to unfold

And if I jump in – from the cliffs
What then?
Shall my splintered bones dance
To memory's sweet light
Or shall I become another shipwreck
On the rocks of infinite possibilities.

Telephone Ring

The bottle lay on its side
Spilling its afterbirth to the floor
Drinking to the sound of the spitting candle
The phone is ringing
When the four minute warning
sounds I shall find you
In the flames

The radio's on
And I understand nothing
Once again
Deft little brushstrokes
More deft than I could ever be
Clichés made into art
Quaint little phrases to satisfy their souls

Did I miss something along the way

Cos I just don't get it

Is this about a girl or a death

The phone's ringing again…
Maybe it's the wrong number
Maybe it's for me
Maybe it's for somebody I used to be
It's probably for somebody I'll never be

I read the news today, oh boy…

The phone's ringing again
Polite conversation
Masturbation
Maybe it's the wrong number
Or maybe it's for me

Marching In Time

The Factories spew out white line
dystopia
Into the moonscape of our minds
The angels sing out for tomorrow's
forgotten memories
As we march in time to the reflections
in the mirror

Ash-cloud indifference circles our
waking moves
In dreams we dance freely
Surrounded by the hushed silence
Of blustered solitary cliff-tops

Memories of memories into
meaningless circles
The distant siren makes me duck into
the passageway
We have been freed to think

But only within the realm of thinking

As the factories spew out their white line dystopia

Rennes-le-Château

I am rooted to the ground like the
trees
And the pale blue mountain backdrop
Is there to tell me where my sky
begins

But they are fake, unreal, improbable
somehow
In their magnificence unlike the
mysteries
And the secrets which they guard
That provide me with meanings just
out of reach
Impossible stories from forgotten
times

Lines in the sand like lines on the
rocks
Are to be both passed and understood

Interpreted and rebuilt into layers
That we attempt to relay to others
But which in truth only reflect back to us
That which we wish to see

Plug Yourself In

Plug yourself in and put your headphones on.
Walk through Paris at daybreak just as the new day is rising. As the orange morning rays triumphantly gash their way through the monuments, over the tenements, and down the sleek tree-lined city streets...Walk hand in hand with the isolation of the music in your ears. The street-life oozes onto the streets, and the morning people brush their sleepy eyes away. Heads numb till the caffeine kicks in; tables on the pavements and the clink of glasses. People shout to each other, wave and smile. But you hear nothing of the street-sounds with your ears; you

simply imagine and allow this imagination to intermingle with the undeviating sounds directed straight into your head via the headphones which make your ears welcome prisoners to the beat. You're a ghost passing by, observing till everyone falls into line – the bus turns the corner along with the change in tempo, and the people and their extraordinary lives begin to move to the rhythms in your head.

A *La Perdrix* Wedding

A *La Perdrix* Celebration
Lovely times of singing rhymes, kicking
off shoes and swaying to the blues
and the reds and the roses and
greens, the oranges and fuchsias and
the sunflower yellows vivid and
brilliant in their standing-proud fields.
The food and the drink and the girls
dressed in pink, the tables and chairs
and sitting in pairs and threes and
fours, sevens and eights and more at
the gate – cars up the street and being
pleased to meet the open-minded
fun-loving kind, liberal and leftie,
artistic and crafty... The bells from the
Church ring right on cue, a throne and
ceremony for the loved and those
present, for the future and happiness,
joy and soulfulness, for the couple and

the friends old and new, for those we
met and those we knew: a shared
moment to take through life, to make
us strong and thrilled and alive. We
were there on that sunny day, we
were there for that week and more –
we cooked and sang and joked and
sang, we laughed and sang and sang
some more – and when the songs we
could sing no more we laughed and
drank to the rising moon, the warming
sun and the loving tune played by the
majestic two who'd gathered us there
to celebrate and share... their love for
each other – and our love for them.
And then we danced

The End of Summer In France

Summer is snatched from our grasp
Screech of brakes, orange glow
Tree-lined avenues, napoleonic sentries
Salute the dusk
Early evening night-time fall
Jokers unfurl their slippers and pack away their headgear

The smell of coffee drinking itself into oblivion
To survive these hibernation times
Multi-coloured descent of crisp arcane imagery
Sudden moves shock the silent
As they wait for longer days
Marble tables cold to the touch
That with an easy swipe of a cloth
Conceal the unrecorded lives of

The easy-boned street life
Would-be intelligentsia
Who smiled and squinted
Only days before
A lifetime ago
As summer is snatched from our grasp

Good Holes

There's a hole in my wall
But I see it as a wall around my hole
Which lets me see out

Maybe if I travel the length of the wall
To one side or the other
Possibly then it will dissolve into nothing

Possibly it will become part of my imagination
Or part of my memory
Or a mixture of the two
One indistinguishable from the other

It is feasible that behind me there is also a wall
Or a hole surrounded by a wall
I have considered this

But I will not allow myself to turn around

I much prefer holes to walls
Even the sound is more… more whole
More inclusive somehow; hole, hole… hole

Unlike wall, which sounds restrictive, Threatening
It sounds like a barrier
… I shall not allow this to overly preoccupy me however

My main consideration these days… huh, these days
In these times, shall we say,
Is that the world, the universe, is made up of holes
My world, my universe, that is
Good holes, I mean
Holes – wide-open spaces surrounded by stuff

You see, essentially we are what we
perceive
And I see the holes
Which, like dots in one of those
paintings
Must be joined together
To make a really big hole
Into which we can all jump
And go:
weeeeeeeeeeeeeeeeeeeeeeeeeeeee

Cool Whispers

I can hear the cool whispered bells
Ringing out the death knell to our
foolish decadence
They will be coming soon
With their horse-whipped hollow
laughter
And their golden invites
Singing songs like waves on pebbles
Brushing over our hypnotic currents
Beckoning us on
To the place we wish not to go
Shadows over snow
The place we fear the most
They will be coming soon
With long fingers and long shadows
I feel their damp echoed breath
Taking hold of me

Sweet mystery of silver-lined
yesterday
Out of reach
With rounded rock and moonlit bay...
And suddenly it is time
The sullen knock
Propels me trance-like to my coat
Collar up I follow my regrets
It is too late to protest
Someone else must now finish my
thoughts
Tidy my desk
And complete my conversations...
I turn, so quickly, as everything has
been
For the final breath on my face
And the withering sun

Notes and Acknowledgements

What the Fuck Happened to Monday, was written when I heard about the death of David Bowie… Brian Eno said that Bowie used to ride the subway in New York pretending to read a Greek newspaper, so as to make people think that he wasn't who he was.

Cool Whispers, I wrote shortly after my father died.

Rennes-le-Château, in France, is a beautiful and strange place steeped in mystery. I can't say I believe the stories of Priests, the Templars and the Holy Grail, but it makes for a good yarn.

Plug Yourself In, I wrote for the cover notes of a friend's and my music album together.

Dalí's House, was written after a visit to Salvador Dalí's house in Spain, summer 2016.

Also by Jean Bonnin

Novels
A Certain Experience of the Impossible
Lines Within the Circle
The Cubist's House

Poetry/Aphorisms/Short Stories
Being and Somethingness
Un-usual Muse-uals

Translations
Magical Sense (by Malcolm de Chazal)
Magical Science (by Malcolm de Chazal)

Edited by Jean Bonnin
The Nuremberg Trials: A Personal History (by Georges Bonnin)

Symbolists believe that art should represent absolute truths that can only be described indirectly. Thus, they write in a very metaphorical and suggestive manner, endowing particular images or objects with symbolic meaning.

V1

www.redeggpublishing.com

www.ingramcontent.com/pod-product-compliance
Lightning Source LLC
Chambersburg PA
CBHW071235090426
42736CB00014B/3096